Let's Get Ready for Earth Day

By Lloyd G. Douglas

Children's Press®
A Division of Scholastic Inc.
New York / Toronto / London / Auckland / Sydney
Mexico City / New Delhi / Hong Kong
Danbury, Connecticut

Photo Credits: All photos by Maura B. McConnell
Contributing Editor: Jennifer Silate
Book Design: Christopher Logan

Library of Congress Cataloging-in-Publication Data

Douglas, Lloyd G.
    Let's get ready for Earth Day / by Lloyd G. Douglas.
    p. cm. — (Celebrations)
    Includes index.
    Summary: A boy describes how his class prepares for Earth Day, by
learning about the holiday from their teacher, preparing and hanging
posters, and planting a tree.
    ISBN 0-516-24262-8 (lib. bdg.) — ISBN 0-516-24354-3 (pbk.)
    1. Earth Day—Juvenile literature. [1. Earth Day. 2. Holidays.] I.
Title. II. Celebrations (Children's Press)

GE195.5 .D68 2003
333.7'2—dc21

                                                    2002009615

Contents

Hi, my name is Dan.

My class is getting ready for **Earth Day**.

My teacher tells us about Earth Day.

She says that on Earth Day, we **celebrate** and care for the Earth.

We make **posters** for Earth Day.

My poster says, "**Recycle**."

9

We put up our posters in the **hallway**.

It is April 22.

Today is Earth Day.

Sunday	Monday	Tuesday	Wednesday	Thursday	Friday	Saturday
		1	2	3	4	
6	7	8	9	10	11	12
13	14	15	16	17	18	19
20	21	22	23	24	25	26
27	28	29	30			

April

13

My class is **planting** a tree for Earth Day.

15

My teacher digs a hole in the ground.

My teacher puts the tree in the hole.

We cover the hole with dirt.

I water the tree.

Now, it will grow.

Happy Earth Day!

New Words

celebrate (**sel**-uh-brate) to do something enjoyable on a special occasion

Earth Day (**urth day**) a holiday on April 22 during which the Earth is celebrated

hallway (**hawl**-way) a way through a building that allows you to pass from one room to another

planting (**plant**-ing) putting something in the ground so that it will grow

posters (**poh**-sturz) large, printed signs that often have a picture

recycle (ree-**sie**-kuhl) to collect something and send it to a special place so it can be used again

To Find Out More

Books
Earth Day
by David F. Marx
Children's Press

Earth Day: Keeping Our Planet Clean
by Elaine Landau
Enslow Publishers

Web Site
Earth Day at Kids Domain
http://www.kidsdomain.com/holiday/earthday/
Learn about Earth Day and fun activities to do on this Web site.

Index

About the Author
Lloyd G. Douglas is an editor and writer of children's books.

Reading Consultants
Kris Flynn, Coordinator, Small School District Literacy, The San Diego County
    Office of Education

Shelly Forys, Certified Reading Recovery Specialist, W.J. Zahnow Elementary
    School, Waterloo, IL

Sue McAdams, Former President of the North Texas Reading Council of the
    IRA, and Early Literacy Consultant, Dallas, TX